MW00743597

STAINED GLASS AT SAMHAIN

Patricia Burke Brogan

Patricia Burke Brogan

salmonpublishing

Published in 2003 by
Salmon Publishing Ltd.,
Knockeven, Cliffs of Moher, Co. Clare, Ireland
web: www.sal monpoetry.com
email: info@salmonpoetry.com

The lines from Patrick Kavanagh's 'A Christmas Childhood' are reprinted by kind permission of the Trustees of the Estate of the late Katherine B. Kavanagh, through the Jonathan Williams Literary Agency.

Registered with Writers' Guild of America East and associate worldwide Guilds.

All rights whatsoever in this play are strictly reserved and application for performance, etc. should be made in writing to the author:
Patricia Burke Brogan, 'Inisfail', 42 College Road, Galway City, Ireland.
Tel/Fax: + 353 (0)91 567684

The moral right of the author has been asserted.

A catalogue record for this book is available from the British Library.

ISBN 1 909992 29 2

Cover etching: *Sean Doras* by Patricia Burke Brogan from *Doras* series of etchings
Back cover photograph: Sarah Fitzgerald
Cover design and typesetting: Siobhán Hutson

Acknowledgments

For their advice and support, I wish to thank: Michael Diskin, Michael Glynn, John O'Donoghue, Michael D. Higgins, Ciarán Parkes, John Kettle, Margaret Faherty, Sheila O'Hagan, Kenny's Bookshop and Art Galleries, The Galway Education Centre, Mary O'Rourke, Members of Galway Writers' Workshop, my husband Edward and members of my family, Brendan, Claire, Theresa and Phil.

STAINED GLASS AT SAMHAIN was first presented by Town Hall Productions at the Town Hall Theatre, Galway City, on October 31st 2002, with the following cast:

Sister Luke	Geraldine Plunkett
Sister Benedict	Darina Ní Dhonnchú
Mother Victoire	Máire Hastings
Father James	Fred McCloskey
The Bishop of Killmacha	Des Braiden
Maura Ber	Susie Lamb

Director	Caroline Fitzgerald
Set Design	Caroline Fitzgerald
	& Patricia Burke Brogan
Lighting Design	Paul Noble
Production Manager	Peter Ashton
Stage Manager	Jane Talbot
Set Construction	Arthur Bell

Stained Glass At Samhain is a work of fiction and any resemblance to people living or dead is purely coincidental.

Stained Glass At Samhain

Time: Halloween. All Souls' Night. Oíche Shamhna, when the boundaries between the living and the dead dissolve.

Location: Interior St. Paul's Convent and Novitiate attached to Mother House and Magdalen Laundry at Killmacha. The buildings are being demolished during the course of the play.

Characters:

Sister Luke, an elderly nun (60 - 70 years)
Sister Benedict, a young white-veiled novice (c. 21 years)
Mother Victoire, Superior of St. Paul's (40 - 50 years)
Maura Ber, a young woman (21 - 27 years)
Father James, the convent chaplain (25 - 30 years)
His Lordship, Bishop of Killmacha (c. 50 years)

The nuns are dressed in veil-coif-guimpe pre-Vatican Two clothing with large black rosary beads and long black leather belts. A row of puppets, dressed as consecrated penitents, sit on a long bench left.

Sound: *Benedictus* from Mozart's *Requiem in D Minor.* Soprano, Alto, Tenor and Bass with Orchestra.

Benedictus qui venit in nomine Domini — Sung by Magdaléna Hajóssyová, Soprano: Jaroslava Horská, Alto: Josef Kundlák, Tenor: Peter Mikulás, Bass. With Slovak Philharmonic Orchestra and Chorus. (Mozart's *Requiem* completed by Sussmayr).

Set: Main image a stained glass window upstage left. Darkness except for faint starlight shining through stained glass window showing Lamentation over the dead Christ or an abstract design. Three cloister-columns of transparent stone-coloured netting hanging at intervals upstage. Broken gothic doorways/cloisters in cotton or linen collaged to the three columns. Stained glass window slightly downstage from cloister-columns. Use of lighting for changing scenes in convent Chapel, Laundry, Bishop's Parlour etc.

A deep trough down front filled with various articles connected with convent and laundry, also bundles of worn-out boots, canvas shoes, linens, aprons, starched guimpes. (The orchestra pit may be used.) A shovel with heap of clay/sand down left. Builders' hard hats.

A 'bier-chair' downstage right near edge of stage on which lies a mummy-like figure wrapped in muslin layers. A small black cross attached to chair above head of figure.

In semi-darkness upstage left/centre behind a column another simple chair.

A dining table, which can be used as Bishop's desk, Bishop's breakfast table and Father James's desk. A carver chair with a number of Sister Luke's guimpes attached (her helicopter). A long bench with 'penitent-puppets' and assortment of baskets, linens and buckets. One small diningroom stool. A thurible and incense holder. Sections of coloured plastics to resemble broken stained glass in drop-box high above stage. Supply of starched guimpes and a simple toothbrush-mug full of soot for Sister Luke's book. A breviary for Father James.

Act 1 Scene 1

Time: Halloween. Oíche Shamhna
Sound: *Benedictus* from Mozart's *Requiem in D Minor. Benedictus in nomine Domini.* Lines repeated by soprano, contralto, tenor and bass with orchestra.

Darkness changes gradually to semi-darkness. Demolition of convent buildings is in progress. Sister Benedict *enters from shadowy cloisters and removes small black cross from above head of the shrouded figure of* Sister Luke, *then moves upstage and places cross in space between cloister columns. Sister Luke stretches her arms, drops black rosary beads to floor with a thud and moves out of gauze shroud wrappings.* Sister Benedict *returns, takes up and folds the layers of shroud, places black rosary beads over folds and moves upstage to sit on chair behind gauze cloister column, where she falls asleep. Copter-chair down left.*

Sister Luke: (*She stands out on stage floor.*)
No birds sing here. Stones and bricks twitch, try to release their trapped horrors. The pain held in the earth. Sister Luke's my name. I had to come back to tell my story. — It's Halloween! Oíche Shamhna! Here in the West there's no boundary between the living and the dead at Samhain! Oíche Shamhna! —
(Sister Luke *unfastens her guimpe tapes and moves towards chair with guimpes attached, her chair-copter.*)
Chapter One. My new book. — Yes. — Yes. I say, yes! — (*Whispers*) I've a hoard of starched guimpes here. — And other treasures. You'll hear all about them later on —
(*Highlight on* Sister Luke *as she sits on chair-copter, dips her finger into a mug of soot and writes on a guimpe. Looks up.*)

You'd wonder why I mix up words, time, days, past and present, the names of my community. Past and present don't matter in God's time. Sure, didn't James Joyce write just like me in his famous Wake! And so does my nephew, the poet. Words — on my heart-shaped guimpes, words already written in the earth, on the surfaces of the Bog of Allen, in the grykes of the Burren, in the flight of birds over Black Head, on drumlins near Monaghan. I catch them, make them visible, write them all down. With soot from that Laundry chimney.

(*Picks up mug of soot.*) — Listen! Those bull-dozers have started up again. —

Sound: Crash of bull-dozed buildings. A portion of cell wall up right collapses.

(*Lights up.*)

SISTER LUKE: Powdered plaster everywhere. Bricks and stones scattered.

(*She stands and moves upstage.*)

That huge chimney — always there with its strange shadows! — Full of soot for my stories. — Pen not needed. My own high window with thickened panes. — But look at this stained glass window here! Half in shadow too. — Can you see the penitential purples and crimsons of the Mother of God, of Mary Magdalene and the women lamenting the dead Christ? — My very, very favourite window.

(*She moves downstage, sniffs.*)

Stench of broken bleach containers. — My resting place — very close to the edge?

(*Moves upstage, lights follow.*)

Sound: Fast convent bell sounds.

Act 1 Scene 2

Lights up

SISTER LUKE: Chapter 2. That sleeping shape up there is Sister Benedict, my other Guardian Angel. Benedict — Bene — dict. — Blessed words.

(Moves downstage and writes. Shadows move as lights dim.)

White-veiled novices take turns to look after me now. — Just in case! — Here take a look at my Magdalen Laundry Halo. A déanta in Éirinn Halo. — Can't you see it? Look!

(She draws a semi-circle with her fingers above her head.)

Sister Benedict, my other Guardian Angel, polishes it up for me every Friday. — Strange place a Novitiate. Never a day dawns, but one of the white-veiled novices is weeping her heart out. Sad, sad stories. Sister Benedict — she'll talk to you later. She's tired out painting banners for the city processions. —

(SISTER BENEDICT exits from cloisters.)

Wouldn't you think they'd take the mothers out of the Laundry and give them their babies from the orphanage, their páistí gréine, instead of popping pennies into black-baby-boxes — for all to see. What does Christ himself think of it? Who has bolted doors and windows on these women? Answer me that!

(Lights change.)

Sound: Demolition sounds.

Act 1 Scene 3

Sister Luke hangs her page-guimpes by their tapes on what remains of cell walls.

Sister Luke: Chapter 3. My life story? First, I must —
(*She hums, Ar maidin moch do ghabhas amach —, as she writes NO DUMPING on a guimpe, attaches it to a post set in the rubble downstage right, returns to chair-copter and sits.*)

Now we're ready!
(*She takes up another guimpe and continues to write.*)

When I was appointed Superior in Killmacha Magdalen Laundry, I changed the so-called penitents' diet. I insisted that they got plenty of milk and fresh vegetables. The finest potatoes, cabbages, onions and herbs grew in our convent garden and we had our own milch cows. I only had to remember my own time in the Novitiate, when the smell of rashers frying for His Lordship's breakfast made me cry with hunger, made me lonely for home.

I spent the Laundry money on the women instead of sending it on to Central Powers. I bought them tennis shoes, I took away their ugly boots, I gave them flowery aprons instead of clay-coloured overalls. —

Come over and look into the crater under that red-toothed bull-dozer.

(*She moves downstage to the 'crater'.*)

Hundreds and hundreds and hundreds of worn-out boots, torn aprons, all holding their own pain! —

I led the women outside to landscape the grounds, to build and decorate my Lourdes Grotto. Mary and Bernadette amidst petunias, arabis and columbines. Our Magdalena and our Katie amidst lupins and Canterbury bells! To let fresh air instead of bleach-fumes into their lungs. Wasn't I right? Wouldn't Christ Himself do the same? — Did I tell you that my sister and myself brought big dowries into the convent with us? Money helps everywhere. Even in a convent.

(*She places another page-guimpe on stage floor as lights change.*)
Sound: Fast convent bell sounds.

Another page for my book! Soon I'll have a tent of story-pages. Like Saint Paul. Saint Paul was a tent-maker. He escaped from his enemies in a basket. Our poor Rosemary tried to get away in a Laundry basket. She wanted to see her baby son in Saint Finbar's Orphanage. When that failed her, she tied bed-sheets together and lowered herself from the dormitory window. We found her next morning. Yes! — Sheets weakened from boiling in the big machines. Her poor neck broken! No, it wasn't suicide! No. That was poor Mary Ann. With a bottle of bleach! Rosemary and Mary Ann were buried over there near that big chimney. Last week the builders exhumed and cremated them — and all the others. — That big chimney? No! No! It's not a crematorium chimney! It's the Laundry chimney! Dust to dust. Into dust thou shalt return. — Mary Magdalene was wronged as well. The crowd, who wanted to get rid of her said she was a great sinner. And she the first witness of the

Resurrection! We'd never have heard about Easter morning only for Mary Magdalene and those brave women. The Apostles ran away! — Ordain women? — The Vatican forbids us to even discuss it! — Shh! But, I must write the truth about those early Christian women. Luckily I've eternity before me! —

(*Sings*):   *Ar maidin mhoch do gabhas amach ar bhruach*
Loch a Léin
An Samhradh teacht 'san chraobh le n-ais
'gus lonnra te ó'n ngréin
Ar taisteal dhom tré bhailte poirt agus bánta
mine ré —

(*Lights low.*)

Act 1 Scene 4

Lights up. SISTER LUKE *picks up another guimpe, but pauses.*

SISTER LUKE: Another Chapter!

We have this new chaplain, Father James. Out of your mind goodlooking! Gorgeous! Over six foot tall. Big grey-blue eyes that'd look through you, dark hair, skin not seminary-looking. A voice deep like a cello. No! More like a double bass. Such a change from nuns' voices.

(She stands, moves to right and chants in soprano tones.)

In nomine Patris, et Filii, et Spiritus Sancti.

*(*FATHER JAMES, *in alb, chasuble and stole, is seen behind stained glass window.)*

FATHER JAMES: *(Chants)* In nomine Patris, et Filii, et Spiritus Sancti.

SISTER LUKE: *(Chants)* Amen!

FATHER JAMES: *(Chants)* Introibo ad altare Dei.

SISTER LUKE: *(Chants)* Ad Deum qui laetificat juventutem meum.

FATHER JAMES: *(Chants)* Judica me, Deus, et discerne causum meam de gente non sancta; ab homine iniquo et doloso erue me. —

(Lights change. FATHER JAMES *exits.* SISTER LUKE *moves downstage.)*

SISTER LUKE: Didn't put on an awwccent like His Lordship. I never took my eyes off you, when you were on the altar, Father James! Custody of the eyes, God forgive me! But God did forgive me. I'll tell you how I know!

(Looks straight ahead)

SISTER LUKE: Sister Benedict came to my cell when I was at death's door, just about to take off! I was screaming at the top of my voice.

(*Screams*) I'm damned, I'm damned for all eternity! I'll go to Hell, because I kept looking at Father James instead of keeping custody of the eyes. —

(SISTER BENEDICT, *wrapped in white sheets, her arms extended like wings, enters from cloisters and stands in space between columns.*)

SISTER BENEDICT:

(*Chants*) I am an Angel sent by God to comfort you, Sister Luke, and to tell you that all your sins are forgiven. The Lord is very pleased with you. He has a place prepared for you at His right hand. Very soon, Sister Luke, I'll take you to Him in Paradise.

(*Exit* SISTER BENEDICT *up left.*)

SISTER LUKE: Sister Benedict didn't really fool me, but I smiled and stopped screeching and roaring. Because, I could see Sister Benedict's own Guardian Angel shining there beside her and smiling at me too. — It's lovely to be able to see Angels. And Archangels.

(*She takes up a page-guimpe, from under her chair-copter*)

My other story? My father was a schoolteacher up North. Why did he move to the south, you ask. A long story to tell you later! Maybe.

(*Lights down.*)

Act 1 Scene 5

Lights low.

Sound: Ticking of clock, then alarm bell.

SISTER LUKE: Chapter 5. There goes Sister Benedict's alarm clock. 5.45 a.m.

(*Highlight on* SISTER BENEDICT *upstage. She wakens, kneels in prayer for a moment and stands up. She lights a candle, fastens the window-locks and turns towards* SISTER LUKE.)

SISTER BENEDICT:

(*Chants*) Benedicamus Domino, Sister Luke!

SISTER LUKE: (*Chants*) Deo Gratias, Sister Benedict! Don't forget to mix toast into my porridge!

SISTER BENEDICT:

Will you come to seven o'clock Mass, Sister Luke? — Please. His Lordship's Mass!

SISTER LUKE: I've work to do here, Sister! Anyway I've been to Father James's Mass! — My new book first. — Still — maybe I'll send along one of my Angels instead! You hurry out, ring the Angelus Bell and open the Big Outside Gates for the vans full of dirty clothes!

(SISTER BENEDICT *exits up right.*)

SISTER LUKE: (*whispers*) She confessed to me that every morning when she opens those Big Outside Gates, she's tempted. Wants to run and run far, far away from this Convent — Only it would hurt her parents. The stigma — their daughter a spoiled nun! A run-away nun! Neighbours gossiping! How many of them gave one day of their lives to work for Big Boss God Himself?

Sound: Angelus tolls above the drone of the river.
Binnng! Binnng!

(SISTER LUKE *moves with arms raised towards the stained glass window*)

SISTER LUKE: Holy Mary Mother of God, pray for us sinners now and at the hour of our death. Amen. Pray for us sinners! Penitents washing. Washing, washing! I did what I could for them. The money the women earned. — It was their own money! The weeks and weeks without sleep, trying to balance the books, staring at pages of figures in my head, scraping through my mind for answers that wouldn't be heard. — But I knew I was right! I knew that things must be changed, if God is going to be allowed to be God!

Central Powers didn't approve of my financial management. — Demoted me! Without warning — 'Be out of this office to-day! Not to-morrow! Get out to-day. Out! Out! To-day!' — But didn't I get the better of them in the end? You'll hear about it all, when Sister Benedict's people publish this book for me.

(*Lights change.*)

Sound: Fast bell sounds.

(SISTER LUKE *sits on chair-copter.*)

I read a lot now. The Book of Job is my favourite. I keep it here in my big pocket and take it out when it suits my situation. Listen to this. Who does it remind you of?

(*She takes a book from the depths of her serge pocket and reads.*)

Even the children look down on me
ever ready with a jibe when I appear.
All my dearest friends recoil from me in horror.
Beneath my skin, my flesh begins to rot

12

and my bones stick out like teeth. —
Job and myself are the best of pals!
(*She draws two stick figures on a guimpe and holds it up.*)
Look at the two of us! Job and Jobess!
(*Lights lower. She writes —*)
Top tables in a supposed 'all are equal'
community! Sometimes when I see that
power-hungry lot at the top table in the
refectory,
(*Moves downstage. Lights up.*)
I run up to the lectern and shout.
Who decided the dimensions of it, do you know?
Who laid its cornerstone
when all the stars of the morning were singing with joy
and the Sons of God in chorus were chanting praise?
Who pent up the sea behind closed doors
when it leaped tumultuous out of the womb,
when I wrapped it in a robe of mist
and made black clouds its swaddling bands;
when I marked the bounds it was not to cross
and made it fast with a bolted gate?
Come thus far, I said, and no farther!
Some of the novices are delighted when I
shout like that.
I can see them smiling under their veils.
But others are either deaf or indifferent.
Minds caged in their starched coifs.
(SISTER LUKE *takes another guimpe.*)

Act 1 Scene 6

SISTER LUKE: Chapter 6. I told you that I was brought before Central Powers, charged with overspending in the Laundry and demoted. They kept me waiting for half an hour outside my own office. — Called me in. Put me facing bright lights. — Lights splitting my brain, scattering my answers, my answers about justice, the rights of women and human rights. They sat in darkness firing questions at me. —

Sound: Other voices over:

The Laundry money? Where are the profits? Profits? Profits? Profits?

SISTER LUKE: A switch went plop in my brain! There and then I made a decision. There and then I decided to escape!

(*Moves quickly across stage.*)

I ran and from that top window beyond the arch. I jumped!

Brought plenty of broken glass with me too! — It was like being a real Angel, broken lights flying through the air. I shouted with joy! Alleluia! Alleluia! —

I landed on the cotoneaster horizontalis over there. Yes. Planted by myself and the penitent mothers. Just a few bruises and a broken anklebone. Bruised in body, not in spirit.

My swollen ankle? Look! (*She shows ankle.*)

I still limp a bit from time to time — Do you remember that famous king, who lived long ago in Thebes? — Oedipus was his name. Oedipus, means swollen foot. Now for ya!

Sure Oedipus and myself might meet one of these days in one of the heavenly mansions! — Central Powers would have locked me away, but because of the size of my dowry, they sent me back to the Mother House on the river. — To be watched over by novices. — Careful, mind my Halo! — I suppose I should have imitated Paul. He used a basket. Not so sure I approve of Paul. Didn't he start the financial arrangements within the institution of the church? In spite of his vision near Damascus. My own patron, Saint Luke, had a softening affect on Paul. I must investigate this sometime!

(*She takes up and writes on another guimpe.*)

SISTER LUKE: Chapter Seven. Joan of Arc. She wanted to defend her Dauphin. So she jumped from Beaurevoir Castle — Jumped from a turret-window sixty feet high. Sixty feet! — They burned her at the stake outside the Cathedral in Rouen, but they couldn't burn her heart. — I'm going to fly to Rouen next week, when I'm on my way to Paris. I've made a helicopter from my guimpes. —

Travel means nothing to me! I flew to the North last week to visit his graveyard. Drumlins edged with whitethorn. A lot of strangers there. — With notebooks! — Foreign accents. — And photographers! If they only knew my story, they'd be taking photos of me! Asking for my autograph! Alleluia! But now, come with me and we'll go back to Killmacha Magdalen Laundry.

(*Lights lower*) I need at least another hundred pages for my book!

(*She moves upstage, searches.*)

SISTER LUKE: That bundle of keys — where is it?

(*Holds up keys.*) Sister Benedict's keys!

Act 1 Scene 7

Use of lighting for scene change.

SISTER LUKE: Now! We'll cross the outside cloister first. —
(Moves behind cloister-columns and out upstage right.)

Careful down these stone steps to the tunnel. —
Very dark in here, smell of damp, no-colour air.
Tunnel air. —

Along through this darkness —

(Moves downstage right to left.)

Unlock this huge door — Lock it carefully
behind us.

(Drops big keys with a bang as she is suddenly highlighted.)

And here we are in Killmacha Magdalen
Laundry! —

(Stands behind row of consecrated penitents.)

Can't you see the consecrated penitents
sitting on that long bench. Crooning lullabies
and cradling their rag-doll babies.

(Lights up a little to show a row of consecrated penitents holding rag-dolls.)

No! They're not ghosts! Can't you see them?
Open your eyes! Listen to them! Hear them? —

(Sings:)   *Seothín seo hó, mo stóir'n, mo leanbh, mo*
sheód gan cealg, mo chuid den tsaol mór.

(Echoed by MAURA BER *backstage. She stares downstage.)*

You never thought about it that way ? — But
you must know! No excuses! No! You're not
too young! — You sent your own dirty filthy
clothes to them! To be scrubbed!

(Enter MAURA BER *up right. She unfolds an old bleached apron,*
pulls it on over her dress. SISTER LUKE *centre stage left.)*

SISTER LUKE:	Maura Ber was only thirteen, still had her schoolbag on her back, when she was brought in here. Isn't that the truth, Maura Ber? — For giving cheek in school! That old bird, your step-aunt Delia beyond in Gort, was jealous of you! And signed you in!
MAURA BER:	(*Centre stage right.*) Every chance I got I studied the building lay-out. For three long years! Then — one night/
SISTER LUKE:	One night, wearing your black canvas shoes, — you climbed that downpipe — tip-toed over this low roof —
MAURA BER:	Up the side of that V shaped roof — over and across the top — jumped across the divide between the Laundry and the convent.
SISTER LUKE:	You slid down on the other side —
MAURA BER:	Another jump into the big field beyond the outer wall. —
SISTER LUKE:	I spent that night in the Chapel praying, praying/
MAURA BER:	There was a new moon and a few stars. Between showers of black rain — I kept running, running!
SISTER LUKE:	My rosary beads cut into my hands as I begged God —
MAURA BER:	I ran west, cross-country to Barnamore. Afterglow from the sun, the Plough, the Milky Way and the North Star guided me. — Then I saw a light in a house off the main road. I knocked on the farm-house door. The farmer's wife gave me a strange look, but the farmer himself said I was like their collie, Bran, the time he strayed in their kitchen door, starving and drowned wet. 'Never a bark out of our Bran! A bad fright he must've got earlier in his life,' said the farmer. She gave me a mug of hot sweet tea and a

salty bacon sandwich. — Fresh bread and real bacon! I'd forgotten what fresh bread and real bacon tasted like. The old collie licked my wet feet, even though I only gave him a few scraps. I was sick with hunger. When the farmer and herself went off to bed, I lay down with my penitent clothes spread out in front of the turf fire. — Couldn't sleep, afraid they'd take me back to Killmacha Magdalen, so I put on my damp clothes, gave Bran a big hug, crept out and away through the night to my cousins beyond Monivea. A few cars passed, but I hid deep in the ditches. — My Step-Aunt Delia never told my cousins and my uncles what she'd done to me! They thought I was in boarding school! — When my real Aunt Brigit in America heard what happened to me, she came over immediately and brought me back to her own home in Boston. Aunt Brigit sent me to college, treated me like one of her own children. I've been back here a few times.

(MAURA BER *stares downstage.*)

But, I could never find that farmhouse afterwards, though I've searched and searched. I wanted to tell the farmer and his wife my true story and to hug Bran again. My Uncle John and my Uncle Gerry and even my granduncle Tom said there was no farmhouse off that road since before the Famine. — Only a few ruins? — I'm going back now to search, search and search. —

(MAURA BER *takes off apron and moves upstage right.*)

SISTER LUKE: (*Facing downstage.*)

Nobody here knows the truth. — I could've stopped her. That night when I was checking

18

the outside doorlocks and taking a look at the stars, the Pleiades and the Milky Way, I saw her climb that drain-pipe and on to that flat roof.

Ah, wasn't I terrified she'd slip and break her neck! — I kept on praying along with her Guardian Angel. Sent my own Angel to help her through the dark. — Her Magdalen Laundry Halo? No! She doesn't wear it! No!

(MAURA BER *exits up right.*)

No! No! Never! Look at Maura Ber now! A graduate in Social History from Harvard!

(SISTER LUKE *moves to right of stage and with* SISTER BENEDICT *carries on table for Bishop's study. Magenta/crimson cover on table with telephone, pens and papers.* SISTER LUKE *sings, Ar maidin moch do gabhas amach etc, until scene is set. Lights low.*)

Act 1 Scene 8

Study in Bishop's Palace. Sister Benedict *exits right.* Sister Luke *sits on chair-copter in low lighting.*

Sister Luke:　A New Chapter!
I'm on a visit to His Lordship's Palace. Look at my wings! No! No! Of course, His Lordship can't see me!

(The Bishop *in Bishop's black soutane with crimson piping, or in black shirt, black trousers with crimson braces, crimson slippers, enters up right, sits at desk, puts on spectacles and checks envelopes. He behaves like an ordinary business man. He lifts telephone.*)

Bishop:　Yes! Yes! Father Matthew! Good morning. You've arranged my trip to Rome? Tickets etc. confirmed? — The trip to Florence too? — Don't forget that visit to Dante's house! — And now reservations — In San Frediano, always my favourite restaurant! Yes — Book the window-table. — Yes! With views of the Ponte Vecchio and the Church of Santa Croce? — Yes! I'll need good Italian cuisine, if I survive the concoctions of those Vatican nuns! — Make sure you have the restaurant and hotel booking confirmed! — For the week! —And a case of wines — My favourite Amarone Alighieri? Yes! — A white too! — A Pinot Grigio '97, of course! And maybe a Chianti, a Classico Riserva '97 — Good! — Now, my ceremonial robes for Rome are your responsibility. The hand-embroidered chasuble and cope. And my decorated mitre!

Don't forget my medicines, the antacids! —
A good supply! My blood pressure medication
also! A second supply, just in case! — Those
Italians might/ — Might send my luggage
to, to — Did you say Siberia? — Hmm! —
Don't be so stupid! — Oh, by the way, that
business in the anonymous letter. — The
one about Father Keaveney seen driving with
a woman? — Have you heard any more?
What? — A young woman? She was trying
to hide, to bend down, when they passed
through Killmacduagh. So — do you think
that? — He was seen in the cinema too?
With her? The same woman? When? —
Not sitting together? I hope not! — Was he
wearing his hat? — No, I mean in the car!
Check this out discreetly. — I know the
letter is anonymous! — His sister or a
cousin! Nonsense! No smoke without a fire
as they say. — I may have to change him —
to a faraway place. — Let me see. — Ah yes!
— A vacancy on an island can be arranged!
— What? — Another letter to-day? — This
one's not anonymous, you say! — Very
serious allegations. Very — On my desk?

(THE BISHOP *reads letter.*)

Very serious indeed! — No, this one's not
about, not about — that woman. — I'll take
this with me to the Vatican. — The
signature is blurred, isn't it? — Keep your
eyes open, Father Matthew! Your ears too!
And your own mouth shut! — You're my
secretary, also my private eye! — No! —
Now, don't forget my antacids! — Yes, I'm
off to the convent. — The usual breakfast,
where I'll be nibbled and chewed by that

Mother Superior with her turned-in-toes. Oh, I almost forgot! Herself and her clutch of nuns will be here, while I'm in Rome. — They insist on changing the wallpaper in my diningroom. — No! — No, not my bedroom! They'll try to soft-talk you into letting them repair my antique footstool! Hide the keys to my bedroom! — No! No! I'll take my office keys with me. Just in case. Don't let them near the cellar! But, above all, keep your eyes and ears open, while they're around! They hear all the gossip. — Of the diocese, I mean! — God bless! No! Hold on! This letter with those vicious allegations. Make a copy for my advisors in the Vatican. — No! No. I'll meet you at my car and put it, the original, into your own hands!

Make one copy, then immediately lock the original in the special safe under my library floor. Start moving now! — Yes, now!

(THE BISHOP *puts down phone. Checks his watch and, taking letters with him, exits.* SISTER BENEDICT *enters and takes off telephone and magenta table-cover. Exits.*)

Act 1 Scene 9

SISTER LUKE: Another guimpe. Another chapter. Chapter 9.
(*She takes up another guimpe and reads from under the collarband.*)

Number twenty-five! My sister's guimpe. She escaped to Paradise last year. The newest postulant got her number. Number twenty-five. Replaced instantly. As if she never existed! Replaced even before she was buried out there under that wee black cross. Recycled! Isn't that the new word for it? —

(*She hides the guimpe under her chair-copter and takes up another.*)

I'll write her life-story another time. — I'm a bit like one of those old monks who wrote the Book of Kells or the Book of Durrow. I wonder should I collect some vegetable dyes from the old convent garden and decorate these pages with the help of quills from seagull wings? I'll ask Sister Benedict to bring me some parsley, onions and beetroot. Colours from the earth — before that builder covers everything with concrete.

(*Lights low.*)

Act 1 Scene 10

Lights up. Bishop's Parlour in convent. MOTHER VICTOIRE *rings a small bell impatiently as she enters up right with lace-edged tablecloth and covers table. She takes a bottle of cognac, brandy glass and box of Havana cigars from hatch up right and arranges them on table. Shadows of nuns may be glimpsed through netted muslin, as they rush and take orders from* MOTHER VICTOIRE, *who is checking china, cutlery etc.* SISTER LUKE *watches.*

MOTHER VICTOIRE:

Has His Lordship arrived, Sister Peter? — Oh, he's getting out of his silver Mercedes — His Lordship's face? — His face! Does he look stern — or happy, or? — Oh, stern! — Has Sister Benedict opened the halldoor yet? — He doesn't like to be left waiting! — She has? — Heat the silver teapot. — Now, I said! — Where's Sister Benedict? — What? What? —

(*Towards kitchen hatch up right.*)

She's gone to the garden for parsley for Sister Luke! Last week it was nettles! — Open the halldoor yourself, Sister Peter! Now! Go! Go! — Sister Philip? — Sister Perpetuo! Yes, you! Have three brown eggs ready to place in the enamel saucepan! — The special saucepan for His Lordship's boiled eggs! — Three, Sister Perpetuo! — Three brown eggs, I said! — Not too small and not too big! — No! Three brown eggs! — Sister Philip, go and find Sister Benedict immediately!

Just go and find her! — Oh, so you're looking after His Lordship's toast! — Send Sister Bernard/Sister Michael/Sister Elphege, Sister/whoever to look for her! —

Wait to put the three eggs into the saucepan until you get the signal from Sister Edward! Sister Bonaventure, you watch on the corridor and give the signal to Sister Jeremiah! —

Voice Over: His Lordship has left the Chapel!

MOTHER VICTOIRE:

His Lordship has left the Chapel? — Right! The toast? The toast! Evenly cooked? Right! Remember one boiled egg, the best and the brownest must go on a linen napkin beside the eggcup! I'll see to the rest! —

The signal? — Now! The eggs! In they go! Two minutes and five seconds before you take them out! —

Your watch has stopped? — Then count, I say! One, two, three. Count! Count! Count!

(THE BISHOP, *in crimson soutane, enters left. As he enters, he looks up, examines the ceiling for signs of dampness, cobwebs etc.*)

BISHOP: Your own ceilings need new paint! And see to those windows! The putty has crumbled!

MOTHER VICTOIRE:

Oh! The ceiling, my Lord? The windows! Yes, my Lord!

(MOTHER VICTOIRE *rushes to kiss* THE BISHOP's *outstretched ruby-ringed hand and ushers him to sit at table. From the kitchen hatch she takes a silver tray on which are a tea-cosy over a silver teapot, a boiled egg in an egg-cup covered by a small embroidered cosy and a silver toast-holder with toast.* MOTHER VICTOIRE *serves tea, boiled egg and toast etc.*)

MOTHER VICTOIRE:

Your breakfast, my Lord.

Bishop: Thank you, Mother Victoire!

(*His Lordship unfolds a linen napkin and covers his soutaned stomach and knees. He takes off the egg-cosy, stares at the boiled brown egg and lifts it up to the light.*)

BISHOP: This egg, Mother Victoire? Look at this crack!

MOTHER VICTOIRE:
Oh, my Lord! I'll ring the kitchen for Sister Perpetuo!

(MOTHER VICTOIRE *fusses and rings small kitchen bell.*)
Another brown egg immediately!

Apologies, my Lord!

Would you care for some ripe Comice pears while you wait? Or would you prefer black grapes?

(MOTHER VICTOIRE *offers a dish of fruit.*)

BISHOP: Just forget the egg and that bell. Sit down! Tell me why nobody in that kitchen is capable of boiling a two-minute five second egg properly.

(MOTHER VICTOIRE *finds a stool and sits at side of table, arms folded, eyes cast down.*)

MOTHER VICTOIRE:
Sister Benedict has a crisis of vocation, my Lord.

BISHOP: A crisis of vocation, Mother Victoire?

MOTHER VICTOIRE:
She insists that she/ Sister Benedict wishes to leave, to abandon the Novitiate, to abandon the Order. Says she/

BISHOP: Why should that interfere with my boiled egg?

MOTHER VICTOIRE:
Sister Benedict always prepares your breakfast eggs.

BISHOP: So she has abandoned the kitchen too?

MOTHER VICTOIRE:
Yes, my Lord!

BISHOP: Sister Benedict! It was a mistake not to allow her home for her mother's funeral Mass. You should have consulted me!

MOTHER VICTOIRE:

> But you were in Florida, my Lord. So, I followed Canon Law. And now she refuses to speak with our new chaplain, Father James, about her vocation. I hoped he might persuade her to persevere. She says her mind is made up this time. She wants to leave immediately. But of course, I told her that permission must come from Rome.

BISHOP:

> Permission from Rome isn't necessary for a novice! You want to frighten her! Isn't that so, Mother Victoire?

MOTHER VICTOIRE:

> We need her in the schools. Especially in the new primary school. She's highly qualified! I'll arrange with the Department of Education for a Mór Fhiosrú before we let her go. But that will take time to set up, my Lord. She's a very good teacher and a favourable report will reflect well on our school!

BISHOP:

> Maybe you've been giving her too much work? Teaching and kitchen work? Her spiritual life may have suffered?

MOTHER VICTOIRE:

> I'll change her from kitchen to sacristy duties immediately! —
>
> Of course, I've put her under obedience.

BISHOP:

> (*Looks directly at* MOTHER VICTOIRE)
> You've put Sister Benedict, a novice, under obedience! Under pain of mortal sin?

MOTHER VICTOIRE:

> Yes! Under pain of mortal sin not to tell anyone about her intention to leave this convent.

BISHOP:

> Hmm! A bit extreme isn't it, Mother Victoire. So there's more to this crisis in the kitchen than a cracked breakfast egg.

MOTHER VICTOIRE:

As you say, my Lord!

(THE BISHOP *takes a Havana cigar from box on table, nips the top, lights up.*)

BISHOP: Will Sister Benedict expect compensation for her work in the schools?

MOTHER VICTOIRE:

According to Canon Law, when she entered she signed away all rights to salary.

BISHOP: But, once she gives you notice, she may insist. Let me see. — Draw up a legal-looking release document. Include a clause signing away of all rights and get her signature before you let her go.

MOTHER VICTOIRE:

Yes, my Lord. Thank you. Of course, we'll compensate you for your help, my Lord!

BISHOP: Yes! Your usual donation for my advice! But, tell me how is the elderly eccentric, Sister Luke?

(*He stands up.*)

MOTHER VICTOIRE:

Sister Luke seems happy to live her own form of spiritual life. She claims to see angels and archangels regularly!

BISHOP: Archangels too! — Do any dark angels, fallen angels visit her?

MOTHER VICTOIRE:

She doesn't say, my Lord.

BISHOP: Strange! Do the novices find it difficult to cope with her?

MOTHER VICTOIRE:

Some do, but Sister Benedict has a special way of managing her, no matter what outrageous notion she takes up.

BISHOP: So, she may react badly, when Sister Benedict leaves the Novitiate?

MOTHER VICTOIRE:

Another problem for me and our congregation — Fresh tea, my Lord?

BISHOP:

No, thank you. I must hurry! Confirmation this morning in Kilmacduagh. Tomorrow a Conference in Maynooth to examine the reasons for falling numbers in our seminaries. The Cardinal expects me to lunch before I leave for Rome next week. And you think you have problems, Mother Victoire!

MOTHER VICTOIRE:

Yes, my Lord. I mean no, my Lord!

BISHOP:

By the way, your new chaplain, Father James — his health? The Tuberculosis? I'll have to report to his cousin, the Cardinal.

MOTHER VICTOIRE:

We take good care of him, my Lord! Plenty of nourishing food. He has put on a little weight.

BISHOP:

At last you've some good news, Mother Victoire! He had a bad time in that seminary. It was reeking with TB. He had a bad time in his first parish too from what I hear. Take care of him!

MOTHER VICTOIRE:

Yes, my Lord.

(THE BISHOP *puts cigar on ashtray and exits up left. Fast bell sound.*)

MOTHER VICTOIRE:

So, Father James is the Cardinal's cousin! — Thank you for letting me know.

(MOTHER VICTOIRE *follows Bishop.* SISTER LUKE *rushes to breakfast table, sits on Bishop's chair and begins to eat the boiled egg, toast, marmalade etc.* SISTER BENEDICT *enters up right, carrying bunch of parsley, which she puts to* SISTER LUKE'*s nose.*)

SISTER BENEDICT:

Oh, Sister Luke! I've been searching for you! In the cloister, the garden, the Chapel.

SISTER LUKE: Would you like some of my cracked boiled egg, Sister Benedict?

(*She offers a spoonful of egg to* SISTER BENEDICT.)

SISTER BENEDICT:
No thank you, Sister Luke! — But, I'll take a little toast. I'm starving.

SISTER LUKE: Eat up, Sister. You can break all the rules now, that you've made your mind up for definite.

(SISTER BENEDICT *stops eating.*)

SISTER BENEDICT:
How do — you — know that?

SISTER LUKE: Herself and His Lordship were talking about you! Don't sign anything!

SISTER BENEDICT:
Don't sign — what?

(MOTHER VICTOIRE *enters up left.*)

MOTHER VICTOIRE:
Sister Luke! His Lordship wouldn't be pleased to see you sitting at his breakfast table, eating his toast/

SISTER LUKE: Would you like some of His Lordship's cracked boiled egg, Mother Victoire? It's delicious! Lovely brown soft-boiled egg — I've put some melty butter in it! Will I mix in some toast too? And some of His Lordship's ashes?

(*She offers a mix of egg, toast and cigar ashes to* MOTHER VICTOIRE, *who stands at a distance.*)

MOTHER VICTOIRE:
Take Sister Luke back to the Noviceship now, Sister Benedict! I'll speak with you later!

(SISTER LUKE *stands, puts a bunch of grapes and a pear into her pocket.*)

SISTER LUKE: For Father James, our gorgeous new chaplain. Alleluia! Alleluia!

(MOTHER VICTOIRE *stares with disgust at the disarray of china and cutlery.* SISTER LUKE *puts pieces of toast into her pocket, drinks tea from Bishop's breakfast cup.*)

SISTER LUKE: Delicious, Mother Victoire! MMyum! Myyumm! I hope you serve our Father James the same special brew? Tastes of — brandy?

(*She takes Bishop's cup and saucer and moves upstage*)

SISTER LUKE: China for Father James! Instead of thick old crockery! Alleluia! Alleluia!

MOTHER VICTOIRE:

Sister Benedict will take you to the Noviceship now, leave His Lordship's china and cutlery in the kitchen, Sister Benedict. It's Beleek Black Label China! I'll see both of you in my office before Evening Prayers.

SISTER LUKE: No, Mother Victoire, I'm much too busy! (*Sings*) *Ar maidin moch do gabhas amach ar bhruach Loch a Léin* —

(SISTER LUKE *takes the kitchen bell, rings it and sings aloud as she exits up left followed by* SISTER BENEDICT.)

MOTHER VICTOIRE:

(*Annoyed*) Forgive us our trespasses — as we forgive those who trespass against us and — lead us not into temptation, but deliver us from evil. Amen.

(MOTHER VICTOIRE *takes a packet of cigarettes from her pocket, checks the cloister outside the Parlour, lights the cigarette and enjoys the smoke, snatches lace tablecloth from table and exits abruptly. Lights down.*)

Act 1 Scene 11

Lights up. FATHER JAMES's *study.* SISTER BENEDICT *enters and places breviary on uncovered table. A plain chair, a table with plain crockery on battered tray, an open harmonium with sheet music on holder, a small bookcase full of spiritual books. Stained glass window showing The Lamentation for the dead Christ. Enter* SISTER LUKE *from cloister up left carrying fruit, china cup and saucer. Pieces of toast in her pocket.*

SISTER LUKE: Father James! Father James!
(SISTER LUKE *puts dishes and fruit on the table. She opens breviary and begins to chant.*)
SISTER LUKE: *Psalm 148 Cosmic hymn of praise.*
                    Alleluia! Let heaven praise Yahweh:
                    praise him heavenly heights,
                    praise him, all his angels,
                    praise him, all his armies!
                    Praise him, sun and moon,
                    praise him, shining stars,
                    praise him highest heavens,
                    and waters above the heavens!
                    Let them all praise the name of Yahweh,
                    at whose command they were created. —
(FATHER JAMES *enters. Both chant together.*)
                    Let earth praise Yahweh;
                    sea-monsters and all the deeps,
                    fire and hail, snow and mist,
                    gales that obey his decree,
FATHER JAMES: *mountains and hills*
                    orchards and forests,
                    wild animals and farm animals,
                    snakes and birds —

SISTER LUKE: Father James! Father James!

FATHER JAMES: Ah, Sister Luke! Good morning!

SISTER LUKE: Alleluia, Father James! Crumbs from the master's table for you.

(SISTER LUKE *takes a piece of toast from her pocket.*)

FATHER JAMES: Pears and grapes — and toast?

SISTER LUKE: From His Lordship's Parlour for your lungs!

FATHER JAMES: Thank you, Sister Luke. For my lungs?

SISTER LUKE: Yes! That seminary you were in! I heard about it.

FATHER JAMES: Oh the seminary? I survived, Deo Gratias! And how are you, Sister Luke?

SISTER LUKE: I'm grand, but sit down and eat before Mother Big Noise comes ballyragging us. Hurry! I brought you a china cup and saucer too! Mother Victoire gives you special crockery. Marked with a secret sign!

FATHER JAMES: For fear of spreading my TB! Same old story! Mary Agnes, the housekeeper in my first parish, did that too. She used gallons of disinfectant on everything I touched in the presbytery! I felt like a leper. (*He sits down.*)

SISTER LUKE: Or like Job himself!

FATHER JAMES: Yes indeed, like Job himself, Sister Luke! It doesn't bother me now. But thank you for the china!

(SISTER LUKE *takes up an open Bible and reads.*)

SISTER LUKE: If I have all the eloquence of men or of angels, but speak without love: I am simply a gong booming or a cymbal clashing.

FATHER JAMES: Paul. Corinthians 13 to/

SISTER LUKE: Paul! The best lines he ever wrote! Can't figure out that man!

FATHER JAMES: Paul was a man with all the weaknesses of a human being, Sister Luke!

SISTER LUKE: Weaknesses of the flesh, you mean. Sting of the flesh he called it. But sure, he was terrified of us, women! Hurry and eat that fruit before Mother Superior Victoire comes to order me out!

(FATHER JAMES *eats grapes.* SISTER BENEDICT *enters from cloister.*)

SISTER BENEDICT:
Sister Luke! Father James!

SISTER LUKE: Tell Father James your news, Sister. He's our Cardinal's cousin!

SISTER BENEDICT:
Please, Sister Luke, come with me.

FATHER JAMES: A distant cousin, Sister Luke.

SISTER LUKE: She can't tell you her secret, Father James! Mother Victoire put her under obedience! A mortal sin if she tells!

SISTER BENEDICT:
Come back to the Noviceship, please, Sister Luke.

SISTER LUKE: Sister Benedict will be taking off her veil soon, Father James.

FATHER JAMES: A — different vocation, Sister Benedict? May the good Lord guide you!

SISTER BENEDICT:
Thank you, Father.

(FATHER JAMES *stands up.*)

FATHER JAMES: I've been waiting for a chance to tell you that I knew your brother, John. We were in the seminary together. He helped me, when I was treating myself for TB. The Reverend Dean wasn't sympathetic and searched my cell regularly, so John allowed me to hide my hypodermic needles and gold medication under loose floorboards in his cell.

SISTER LUKE: Gold medication, Father James? Gold? You're full of gold!

(SISTER LUKE *touches* FATHER JAMES'*s shoulder.*)

FATHER JAMES: Yes, gold saved many lives before the new drugs were discovered, Sister Luke. But, Sister Benedict, your brother would have been expelled instantly, if the Reverend Dean found the needles and medication. Me too! Out! Out! Out instantly! Though the Reverend Dean had recovered from TB himself.

SISTER BENEDICT:
John often spoke about the Dean. Hard times.

SISTER LUKE: If I have all the eloquence of men or of angels, but speak without love, I am simply a booming gong or a clashing cymbal.

FATHER JAMES: The Dean didn't find out, Deo Gratias. I got through my medical, X-rays were clear and I was ordained.

SISTER LUKE: And Mary Ag., the housekeeper with the buckets of disinfectant. Wait 'til you hear this, Sister Benedict!

FATHER JAMES: (*To* SISTER BENEDICT) Mary Agnes, poor thing, was terrified the Parish Priest would pick up TB from me. I had to walk over a mat doused in Dettol, when I left my bedroom. The presbytery, my food, my clothes, my shoes smelled of Dettol. I don't know what the parishioners made of it. Mary Agnes was very curious too. When I was out on parish duties, she went through my desk, wardrobe and chest-of-drawers. Wearing her rubber gloves, of course! — But, I learned to put fine cotton threads across cabinet and desk openings. So I knew when she had visited my room with her rubber gloves. There's none so quare as folk, Sister Luke!

(MOTHER VICTOIRE *enters up right.*)

MOTHER VICTOIRE:
So, now you're annoying Father James, Sister Luke! Didn't I tell you to go to the Noviceship!

Sister Luke: Father James was telling us about strange and curious people.

Mother Victoire:
Take that china back to the kitchen now, Sister Benedict.

Sister Luke: I'll help you, Sister Benedict. Goodbye, Father James. Don't let them put the dalladh mullóg on you, Father James! Strange and curious people!

(*Sings as she gathers dishes with* Sister Benedict *and exits up right.*)
Ar maidin mhoch do gabhas amach ar
bhruach Loch a Léin —

(Mother Victoire *watches as* Sister Benedict *exits followed by* Sister Luke. *She moves around the small parlour and touches ledges with her fingers and examines her fingers for dust.*)

Mother Victoire:
Father James, I'd like you to speak with Sister Benedict. She's in a crisis of vocation and needs spiritual advice.

Father James: Certainly, Mother Victoire! Her vocation? There are so many kinds of vocation. The Holy Spirit may have other plans, other work for Sister Benedict.

Mother Victoire:
Just advise her to persevere!

Father James: I'll listen to what she has to say.

Mother Victoire:
Thank you, Father James! — I see that Sister Luke has been annoying you!

Father James: Not at all, Mother Victoire! Sister Luke and I get on very well.

Mother Victoire:
I hope we don't have to put her in — a Rest Home, Father James, now that Sister Benedict may leave us. The doctors say Sister Luke's brain is rotting away!

FATHER JAMES: Rotting away! But, Sister Luke is saner than most of us, Mother Victoire! We miss the many splendoured thing.

MOTHER VICTOIRE:
You think so?

(FATHER JAMES *coughs.* MOTHER VICTOIRE *recoils.*)

MOTHER VICTOIRE:
Indeed, Father James!

(MOTHER VICTOIRE *exits.* FATHER JAMES *opens his breviary, walks to and fro, stops to stare at stained glass window, then continues to walk and read breviary. A convent bell rings. He moves back to stained glass window.*)

FATHER JAMES: Yes, Sister Luke, you've summed it all up! I am but a booming gong, a clashing cymbal.

(*He stares at the stained glass window.* SISTER LUKE *enters up left with a mug of tea.*)

SISTER LUKE: Fresh tea, Father James! The Booming Gong herself is lecturing them in the kitchen, God help us!

(FATHER JAMES *takes up the mug and looks at the stained glass window.*)

FATHER JAMES: Thank you, Sister Luke! All made of clay, whether it's china or rough pottery. All come from the earth. Like glass, clear or stained. (*Prays*) But now, O Lord, Thou art our Father. We are the clay and Thou our potter and we all are the work of Thy hand.

SISTER LUKE: Isn't it lovely, Father James? My beautiful stained glass window!

FATHER JAMES: Watch the light coming through those crimsons and ultramarines, Sister Luke!

(SISTER LUKE *moves to the window and both stare at the window. They are enveloped in colour.*)

FATHER JAMES: In La Chapelle on Ile de la Cité in Paris! Walls of stained glass off-set royal purples over sculpted apostles and marble floors.

SISTER LUKE: In Paris.

FATHER JAMES: Centuries ago master glaziers dreamt up new colours for that huge Reliquary.

SISTER LUKE: A huge Reliquary.

FATHER JAMES: For His crown of thorns, His splintered cross. From Golgotha to Constantinople for King Louis and Blanche of Castile.

SISTER LUKE: A huge Reliquary in Paris.

FATHER JAMES: Over eight hundred years ago.

SISTER LUKE: For His crown of thorns.

FATHER JAMES: His splintered cross.

SISTER LUKE: In Paris.

(*He moves towards* SISTER LUKE.)

FATHER JAMES: One Holy Saturday night we students kept watch for Easter dawn. — The stone mullions dissolved in colour. — I hope to return to Paris some time —

SISTER LUKE: To Paris.

FATHER JAMES: Yes, Sister Luke!

(*He takes breviary from table.*)

SISTER LUKE: Paris! I'd like to see Paris!

Sound up: *Agnus Dei* from Mozart's *Requiem in D Minor*
LINES:
Agnus Dei qui tollis peccata mundi, miserere nobis.
Agnus Dei qui tollis peccata mundi, miserere nobis.
Agnus Dei qui tollis peccata mundi, dona nobis pacem.

Sung by soprano, alto, tenor and bass with orchestra.

(*Colours swirl as lights come down gradually.*)

Interval
(Optional)

Act 2 Scene 1

Lights up.

SISTER LUKE *moves downstage as she writes.*

SISTER LUKE: Chapter Sixteen.

(MAURA BER, *in American college clothes, enters from cloisters up right and moves towards* SISTER LUKE.)

SISTER LUKE: Ah, Maura Ber! Did you find that farmhouse and the people who gave you shelter?

MAURA BER: No, Sister Luke! But, I won't give up that search! I'll go on!

SISTER LUKE: You'll find them. No boundaries between them and us during Samhain!

MAURA BER: I hope you're right, Sister Luke. But could you help me, please? I need more stories about the laundries for my post-grad thesis in Harvard. The women won't talk to me, pretend they never met me. Chrissie and Magdalena just look through me.

SISTER LUKE: They want to pretend it never happened, Maura Ber. — But it's always there deep down. Like a dark stain. — Oozing. — Oozing. — This morning I thought about it again.

(SISTER LUKE *moves to chair-copter.*)

MAURA BER: Tell me, Sister! Please! I need inside stories.

(MAURA BER *takes a small tape recorder from her portfolio.*)

MAURA BER: Do you mind if I record you?

SISTER LUKE: Of course not.

(SISTER LUKE *sits on chair-copter.* MAURA BER *finds a small stool under table and sits close to* SISTER LUKE.)

SISTER LUKE: When I was first appointed Superior of Killmacha Laundry — just before your time there, Maura Ber — one evening a young cow escaped from the abattoir across the road and ran in through our Big Gates. She must have smelled the blood flowing from that slaughterhouse. Animals haven't lost their sensitivity like us humans — I could smell her fear. Pakie-Joe, the gardener, tried to stop her, but, head up and bawling fiercely, she came straight for me. I screamed at Pakie-Joe not to use the spade on her. Just then the Angelus Bell rang. She turned and raced up the graveyard slope towards our Grotto. When the van-men followed, she bolted and charged down against the cut-stone of the Chapel. Burst open her poor arteries! — Never saw so much blood in my life! I couldn't look, when the van-men took the poor thing away. — I'll never forget the fear in her eyes!

MAURA BER: Oh, no! No!

SISTER LUKE: The only time I saw so much blood-loss was when Julia-Ann Moran aborted her baby. In the big bathroom. With a wire clothes-hanger. —

(MAURA BER *covers her face with her hands.*)

SISTER LUKE: Julia-Ann was never the same in the head after that. A walking-dead woman. — I could never find out where her baby is buried. Not in consecrated ground anyway!

I had to fight with Central Powers to get Julia-Ann herself buried in blessed ground. She was buried over there under that broken-down limestone. That was before those builders caused them to be exhumed and cremated. All those women! Come over with me and I'll show you. — There must be body-parts still here after the bulldozers.

MAURA BER: Body-parts, Sister?

SISTER LUKE: How could the bull-dozers take all? Every scrap of bone? Sinew? — Heart? Everything? — And I know for certain that their souls come back at Samhain. I'm certain! Come over here!

(*Lights down as* MAURA BER *and* SISTER LUKE *move towards right centre stage. Dark shadows move across stage.* MAURA BER *bends down and picks up a battered medal. She cleans it off.*)

MAURA BER: Look, Sister Luke! An old medal — It must belong to one of the women who — ?

(SISTER LUKE *takes the medal and examines it.*)

SISTER LUKE: Yes! It's a medal — That's Katie's medal of the Little Flower. Yes. Katie's medal. She used to wear it on a blue string around her neck. She said it smelled of roses. It covered up the Laundry smells. The Little Flower, Saint Thérèse, Carmelite nun. When she performs miracles, she fills the air with the perfume of roses.

MAURA BER: The Little Flower! I gave up all that religious stuff long ago.

SISTER LUKE: You think it's superstition, don't you, Maura Ber?

MAURA BER: There's a very fine line between this stuff and superstition!

SISTER LUKE: Bud forth as the rose planted by the brooks of waters: give ye a sweet odour as frankincense. Send forth flowers as the lily and yield a smell and bring forth leaves in grace and praise with canticles and bless the Lord in his works. From Ecclesiasticus 39, Maura Ber! Little Thérèse wanted to be ordained a priest. Had her hair cut in tonsure like a priest.

MAURA BER: No! What woman would want to be a priest? Priests are the new outcasts!

SISTER LUKE: Even so, many women really want to be ordained. Poor Little Thérèse suffered a lot.

She died of TB in her convent at Lisieux. On her deathbed, she was almost in despair, plagued with disbelief, couldn't pray, was surrounded by phantoms of night instead of Angels! My madness is to hope, she said. — Just like most of us! — I must visit Lisieux on my way back from Paris. And have a little chat with her.

MAURA BER: So you're off to Lisieux and Paris, Sister Luke?

SISTER LUKE: Yes! And Rouen too for advice from Joan of Arc! In my new helicopter!

(SISTER LUKE *moves to chair-copter and sits down.* MAURA BER *follows her.*)

MAURA BER: But, what about Katie, the woman who wore this medal? Tell me more.

SISTER LUKE: Our Katie dropped dead on to a wheel-barrow of manure, when she was cleaning out the cow-byres. That medal was buried with her.

(SISTER LUKE *puts the medal to her nose. Breathes in, then offers it to* MAURA BER. MAURA BER *puts the medal to her nose and inhales.*)

SISTER LUKE: Can you smell the roses, Maura Ber?

MAURA BER: Roses? No. Just clay smells.

(SISTER LUKE *holds medal to her heart.*)

SISTER LUKE: The bed of heaven to you, Katie!

MAURA BER: May I keep the medal, Sister? Please? For my archives.

SISTER LUKE: Of course, Maura Ber.

(*They both examine the medal.* SISTER LUKE *gives medal to* MAURA BER.)

MAURA BER: Thank you, Sister! But, Katie's story? — Where did she come from? — Why was she abandoned in this place?

SISTER LUKE: Katie was a country girl. Strong boned. Sad, sad eyes. She used to do a weather forecast for me — from the clouds and the wind, whenever I took the women out to work on the rockery around the Grotto. She could handle a spade better than Pakie-Joe, our gardener. Katie had names for all the cows. Daisy, Bluebell, Flossie and the like! She sang lovely songs for them. I Dreamt I Dwelt in Marble Halls and Gortnamona —

Sound: Echoing of song *I Dreamt I Dwelt in Marble Halls* to end of scene.

MAURA BER: My granduncle Tom used to sing Gortnamona and Beidh Aonach Amáireach i gContae an Chláir.

SISTER LUKE: Yes! Katie held long conversations with the cows. — But I noticed that she didn't talk much with the other women. Not real talk.

MAURA BER: Did she ever try to escape?

SISTER LUKE: Escape? Hhm! Pakie-Joe always brought the cows to the byres inside the high walls. He was always around, had an eye like a hawk. She wouldn't have gone far before he'd pounce! — By the time I was appointed here, Katie had become a consecrated penitent and had lost the will to escape.

MAURA BER: Poor Katie. Institutionalised. What was her surname?

SISTER LUKE: Katie —? Katie —? Oh. Lord, I can't remember. — There were so many in the Laundry. — No real records. But now that you have her medal, she'll never be forgotten.

MAURA BER: Thank you, Sister Luke.

(MAURA BER *holds up the medal.*)

Oh, thank you! Katie'll never be just a heap of dust. I'll see to that. Her story will be published in my thesis. — Did any of her family come to her funeral?

SISTER LUKE: No.

MAURA BER: Anyone from outside?

45

SISTER LUKE: Nobody came. — Nobody. — Though, a strange thing happened as we walked, just the few of us, in Katie's funeral procession. All the cows in that outside field raced over to the high wire fence. They stood together and began to moan and ologón.

MAURA BER: They knew?

SISTER LUKE: They were all black cows, Maura Ber. So strange to see that black chorus of cows ululating and mourning until Katie's body was buried out of sight.

MAURA BER: So she was buried here, Sister? And that builder cremated her with all the others. But now Katie won't be forgotten. Ever!

Sound: Up a little *I Dreamt I Dwelt in Marble Halls.*

(MAURA BER *and* SISTER LUKE *examine the medal again.* SISTER LUKE *puts it to her nose, inhales, gives it to* MAURA BER. MAURA BER *pauses, but remains silent, moves away towards exit up right, then turns to* SISTER LUKE *with an astonished expression on her face. Highlight on* MAURA BER.)

SISTER LUKE: May the road rise with you, Maura Ber!

Sound: *I Dreamt I Dwelt in Marble Halls.*

(*Dark shadows as* MAURA BER *exits.*)

Act 2 Scene 2

Lights up show sacristy with vestments, albs, chasubles, soutanes, surplices, copes, etc. hanging in an open wardrobe up centre. A chest of wide drawers down right with the following labels, Altar Cloths, Communion-rail Cloths, Corporals, Purificators, Tabernacle Covers, Palls etc. Can be simplified. A carved prie-dieu centre left.

Open door into Chapel up left shows part of main altar over which a sanctuary lamp glows.

SISTER BENEDICT, *her white veil pinned back from her face, enters from convent Chapel carrying a thurible. She places the thurible and a small basket, which holds a variety of cleaning and polishing cloths, on the table. She reads from a list of duties and checks them off with a pencil. Low lights on* SISTER LUKE *centre right.*

SISTER BENEDICT:

Duties for to-day, Sister Benedict! Set the main altar for Festive Mass. Yes! Check lace cloths on side altars. Yes! Check cloth on communion rails. Yes!

(Stops reading.) Why has Mother Victoire changed me from kitchen duties? So suddenly! Did she find out that I switched dinner-plates in the refectory? Does she know that I've been giving her fillet steak to Sister Luke? Did one of the novices see me changing the plate-covers? — But I was so careful! — Oh, yes! Somebody reported me! — Still, I'm glad I did it! Sister Luke is so fragile, so pale. She needs extra nourishment. Yes! I'm glad I did it!

(Looks out towards altar.)

Yes! I'm glad I changed the plates around!
But what's going to happen to Sister Luke now?
Oh, God! Oh, God! —

(*Reads from list of duties.*)

Replace the ribbons in the Missal for the
special Feastday.
Yes, I will! Yes! —
Clean and polish the handbasin. Finished!
Polish the sanctuary lamp and refill with oil.
Done.
I didn't break any kitchen dishes, though I
did eat a scrap of Mother Bursar's special
Christmas-cake. I was so hungry! Mea culpa!
I'll confess and do my penance.

(*She sets out the Mass vestments. She opens the large Missal, fixes
the ribbons. Takes up list and pauses.*)

SISTER BENEDICT:

'Permission from Rome', said Mother
Victoire. When will my release letter come?
Six months now. Waiting, waiting, waiting.
Waiting for some faceless Vatican official in
some musty office to sign a piece of paper to
allow me to go home.

(*Holds up list*) In Latin, I suppose! Or Italian! Gratie Mille!
What can he know? How can he know why
I can't stay? That I must go home to try to
say goodbye to my dead mother. I'm sure
His Holiness, the Pope, would understand!
— Wouldn't he? — Wouldn't he? — Last
time I saw her — sitting in her garden — the
roses and lupins she had planted with so
much love were bursting into bloom. She
was wasting away. Wasting away with cancer!
Her eyes huge with pain. 'See you soon,
Mom' — I promised as I left her — to
return here to this place, this Novitiate. —

48

Those last five weeks — of her agony — I should have gone home, walked out without permission!
Straight out the hall door! I should have! I should have! Should've been with her and Dad. — To cool her with iced-water, — to wipe the deathsweat from her forehead. — To pray with her on her last journey. — My mother enclosed in a coffin being lowered into, into — into — that — How can that stranger in the Vatican know or understand? Soon, Mom, I'm — going — home to sit in your garden, — to walk to the cemetery, to stand by your — grave. — But, now I'll never be able to really say goodbye to my own mother! How can I?

(Turns towards stained glass window.)

Help me, Lord! You could have healed her! Why didn't you? — Why? Why? You must understand! You must! Help me! Help me! — Oh, God! Oh, God!

(Reads from list.) Prepare for Benediction! Polish thurible. Refill incense holder.

(She pours incense into holder and begins to polish thurible. FATHER JAMES *knocks at sacristy door and enters).*

FATHER JAMES: Good morning! Good morning, Sister Joachim! Oh, — Sister Benedict? Sorry! Where's Sister Joachim?

(SISTER BENEDICT pulls her veil forward and keeps custody of the eyes.)

SISTER BENEDICT:

Good morning, Father James! Sister Joachim has been changed to kitchen duties. Shall I light the Mass candles now, Father James?

FATHER JAMES: Not yet, Sister! I see you're polishing the thurible! Speaking of thuribles — In his last letter your brother told a wonderful story.

SISTER BENEDICT:
> Oh, did he! How is he? Tell me!

FATHER JAMES: He's really very well! Doing splendid work in Japan. Near Nagasaki. He expects to be home for a break in Springtime. You didn't hear?

SISTER BENEDICT:
> No! Our letters are censored, Father James.

FATHER JAMES: I didn't know that!

SISTER BENEDICT:
> Springtime. Very good news!

(FATHER JAMES *holds up thurible.*)

FATHER JAMES: Yes! It is good news indeed! But wait until I tell you the story! When the builders were preparing the foundations for a new Cathedral on the site of the bombed Cathedral of Nagasaki, what did they find amongst the rubble and nuclear waste? They found — a charred, but otherwise perfect thurible. Devastation. Desecration. 70,000 humans incinerated, many thousand sickened with radiation and one small thurible survived the plutonium horror! And that thurible is still being used for ceremonies in the new Cathedral of Nagasaki. The ways of war — to the ways of peace. Deo Gratias!

SISTER BENEDICT:
> 70,000 humans incinerated, many thousand sickened with radiation and one small thurible survived the plutonium horror!

(*Looks straight at* FATHER JAMES.)
> Deo Gratias?

FATHER JAMES: Ohh — I didn't mean it like that, Sister!

(*He checks his watch.*)
> Now I must prepare for Mass, Sister.

(*He places thurible on table, kneels at prie-dieu, opens breviary and prays silently.* SISTER BENEDICT *lights a taper and moves towards Chapel.* SISTER LUKE *hurries over to* FATHER JAMES.)

SISTER LUKE: Father James! Father James! Tell me that story again! For my book!

FATHER JAMES: After Mass, Sister Luke! Certainly!

SISTER LUKE: But, but my book! My book!

FATHER JAMES: After Mass, Sister!

(SISTER BENEDICT *points to altar and places her finger on her lips for silence.*

SISTER BENEDICT *moves into Chapel.* FATHER JAMES *resumes his prayer.*

Lights dim. Mass bell tolls.)

Sound up: Nóirín Ní Riain sings solo with shruti box: *Kyrie eleison, Christe eleison* from *The Greatest Ornament* – Liturgy 11th to 12th centuries. Repeat solo and continue to male choir. Or *The Alleluia Magnificat.*)

Act 2 Scene 3

Lights up show SISTER LUKE *walking through cloisters and moving to attach extra starched guimpes to sides and back of her chair-copter.*

SISTER LUKE: Wasn't that a gorgeous Mass! They were all there! All the VIP Saints with their books, Matthew, Mark, Luke and John. Luke, who was painting a lovely picture of Our Lady, gave me a great big hug! Paul raised one eyebrow and half-smiled at me. Francis's Halo was humming with goldfinches. Colmcille had The Book of Kells under one arm. Patrick read from his Breastplate. Thérèse held up her Story of a Soul and down floated a shower of lovely pink roses! And then there was Brigit in all her glory right beside The Bishop! Wearing her own mitre and crozier and her long flowing cloak. But The Bishop was silent, when Magdalen sang The Magnificat as she carried an amphora of spikenard to the altar steps.

Sound: *Magnificat cum Alleluia* sung by Nóirín Ní Riain.

Even the cast-out saints arrived.

The demoted saints, Philomena, Christopher and Veronica.

And Angels! Ten thousand times ten thousand of them and thousands and thousands! Our Father James sang in Latin and blessed us with the thurible full of burning incense. God Himself smiled and smiled.

(She walks around her chair-copter.)

And here's my new helicopter! New wings!

New journeys!

Do you know that when President Kennedy came to Ireland, he flew overhead in his big green helicopter.

Flew right over us here! (*She lifts her arms.*) Such a gorgeous tan, such shining white teeth! Very like our Father James. — Though not — quite — as good-looking!

(SISTER LUKE *stands behind chair-copter.*)

President Kennedy promised to come back to visit us again, but his enemies blew his lovely brains to bits in Dallas.

(*Enter* MOTHER VICTOIRE *with a letter.*)

When I get back from Paris, my next trip will be to the United States of America and I'll drop in on him. — And we'll have a nice cup of tea!

(SISTER LUKE *fastens another guimpe to her chair.* MOTHER VICTOIRE *stares in amazement at* SISTER LUKE.)

MOTHER VICTOIRE:

Well, Sister! You seem to be busy! Where's Sister Benedict?

SISTER LUKE: She's doing her penance! On her knees scrubbing the long corridor!

(MOTHER VICTOIRE *checks her pocket-watch.*)

SISTER LUKE: Very soon I'll be off to Paris with Father James. To see the stained glass of La Chapelle, of Notre Dame and Chartres! Alleluia!

(MOTHER VICTOIRE *stares at* SISTER LUKE, *makes sign of the cross and exits quickly.*)

SISTER LUKE: Au revoir, Mother Victoire!

Notre Dame on Holy Thursday.

The washing of feet, the anointing, the breaking of bread!

And La Chapelle to wait for Easter morning.

(SISTER LUKE *sits in chair-copter.*)

SISTER LUKE: But before I take off, I want to tell you something. My parents owned a drapery shop on the main street of Ballymore. Rolls of linens, cottons, flannels. Skeins of coloured wools. Hats with ribbons and feathers. Mens' suitings of frieze and corduroy. I can still remember the warm clothy smell of our shop. —

We were nice and comfortable at home. That's why my sister and I brought such big fat dowries with us, when we entered the convent on the river. Cash's name-tapes sewn on our trousseaux linens and bath sheets. Foxford blankets folded in tissue paper with muslin bags full of lavender packed into cabin trunks.

Sound: A reel, *The Limestone Rock* played by Micho Russell.

My father taught us the melodeon and the tin whistle. His father, my grandfather, taught him. —

(*Sound of tin whistle continues.*)

I used to hide under our diningroom table when we had guests at home! —

One day a big man with a funny accent came to our house. He was tall, with a thin white face and piercing eyes. Under the table I made sure not to go near his big rough boots.

(*Fade sound of tin whistle.*)

He said, 'I'm a cobbler, I make and mend boots!' and he told Daddy that his own mother had died and was buried up North. —

He kept on saying to Daddy, 'You're my real father!'

Mammy began to cry. Daddy told the man to go away and not be telling lies. —

But the man kept on saying, 'You're my real father!'

Mammy fainted and Daddy took her out to the kitchen. Then Daddy came back, took a bundle of money from the safe hidden behind the big picture over the fireplace and said, 'Promise me that you'll never come back to this house again!'

The man took the money. His last words were, 'She's buried with your other son, my twin brother, in the cold Northern clay!' —

Mammy always had tears in her eyes when she asked Daddy about the man from the North.

'Why didn't you tell me about that woman? Did you love her? Was she beautiful?'

'She had lovely golden hair' was all he'd ever say. —

I could see the ghost of that woman from the North in every fair-haired penitent in The Laundry. —

That's my story. Alleluia.

(*She takes another guimpe, dips her finger in soot.*)

I often wonder what Christ wrote in the sand about the Pharisees, who wanted to stone that poor woman to death.

(Sister Luke *in chair-copter as lights fade.*)

Sound: Demolition of buildings.

Act 2 Scene 4

THE BISHOP *can be seen kneeling in the sanctuary near the stained glass window.* SISTER LUKE *is sitting on her chair-copter.*

SISTER LUKE: Did you know that His Lordship is terrified of flying? He looks very worried! Doesn't he? The Poor Bishop! There he is praying for a safe journey to the Vatican! — Yes! — I'll ask him if he'd like a trip in my new helicopter. Just the two of us up there like real stars. I'll fly him straight to Rome, cruise above the Via Aurelia Antigua, get a bird's eye view of the stone Angels guarding the fortress and land him right in the middle of St. Peter's Square. In full view of Michelangelo's masterpiece! No airport queues, no security checks, no monitor-watching, no waiting in make-shift boxes.

(THE BISHOP *stands up and moves towards* SISTER LUKE, *who has moved upstage.*)

Yes my Lord! And you can smoke your own Havana cigars! Much safer than Sir Anthony's private jet with all that talk of big financial deals. Sure couldn't I signal to St. Peter and His twelve Apostles to hold their fishing nets up high, like safety nets, just in case of turbulence on our arrival. Turbulence from the Curia, I mean! I myself could slip by all those handsome Swiss Guards and drop into the Vatican Grottoes under the Basilica for a long chat with my favourite Italian, Pope John the Twenty-Third. I'll try to console him.

The poor darling is very disappointed that his Aggiornamento of Vatican Two was never accepted here in our Island of Saints and Scholars.

(THE BISHOP *becomes very stern, as* MOTHER VICTOIRE*, holding a document, rushes from the cloister. She stops suddenly.*)

And then to our lovely smiley Pope John Paul the First, who only survived in the Vatican for thirty-three days. — I'll bring him bundles of fresh herbs from our garden, make him a good strong cup of my own parsley and fennel tea. Instead of that morning brew that killed him. I'll make him smile again, the poor darlin'! — No Roman holiday for me, but straight back over the Alps to Paris and La Chapelle, my own favourite place, Alleluia!

(SISTER LUKE *moves closer to* THE BISHOP *and tries to take hold of his cape.* MOTHER VICTOIRE *tries to make* THE BISHOP *focus on the document.*)

MOTHER VICTOIRE:

My Lord, that legal release document for Sister Benedict! Your generous advice, please.

(THE BISHOP *ignores* MOTHER VICTOIRE *as* SISTER LUKE *brings him to her chair-copter.*)

SISTER LUKE: Fasten your seatbelt, my Lord Bishop of Killmacha! Ready for take-off to St. Peter's! I guarantee you a gorgeous view of all those Italian vineyards from my brand new helicopter!

(THE BISHOP *pulls back.*)

SISTER LUKE: Not — ready — for take-off, my Lord? — A big strong man like yourself — afraid! — But, doesn't His Holiness himself love flying around the globe? I'm certain he'd be delighted to travel with me in my gorgeous helicopter! Look! Look!

(THE BISHOP *moves back a little more.*)

> Oh, you've never trusted helicopters either!
> Sure, didn't that famous Italian artist,
> Leonardo da Vinci, make the very first
> helicopter? And wasn't he a pure Italian?

(MOTHER VICTOIRE *stands in front of His Lordship. They move upstage.*)

MOTHER VICTOIRE:

> Now you see for yourself, my Lord!

SISTER LUKE: His Lordship is lost for words! He has no
imagination, the poor man! — No, I'm in no
hurry to go to Rome myself! What was the
name of that wise man who said, that if you
don't bring God with you to Rome, you
won't find God there!

(SISTER LUKE *returns to her chair-copter as* THE BISHOP *and* MOTHER VICTOIRE *walk through the cloisters. We see, but cannot hear them as they discuss the document.*)

SISTER LUKE: Look at the two of them! Magpie and Peacock!
But she'll never succeed in dominating him!
Now I can fly straight to my very own La
Chapelle. Alleluia!

(*Lights low. Demolition sounds.*)

Act 2 Scene 5

Lights up. More guimpes spread on floor around chair-copter.

SISTER LUKE: I'm just back from La Chapelle. I'll tell you all about it in my next book. Takes time to let it all sink in.

(SISTER BENEDICT *enters from cloisters carrying a bundle of starched guimpes.*)

SISTER BENEDICT:

I won't need these guimpes anymore, Sister Luke.

(SISTER BENEDICT *kneels and gives bundle of guimpes to* SISTER LUKE.)

SISTER LUKE: Oh, Sister Benedict, more pages for my books! Thank you, thank you!

SISTER BENEDICT:

I've come to say goodbye, Sister Luke. I'm leaving. I'm going home. This evening.

SISTER LUKE: You're — going — home? — Home? Did you sign that document?

SISTER BENEDICT:

Yes, Sister Luke. I'd sign anything at this stage! Anything! I'm not interested in compensation! My Dad and my sister are coming to collect me at six o'clock! They're delighted! — Oh but, Sister Luke, — Mother Victoire says she — may send you to — a Rest Home — when I've left — the convent. I'm really very sorry, Sister Luke.

SISTER LUKE: Rest Home? Mother Victoire wants to dump me in an asylum! Ah! — But she doesn't guess my secret.

SISTER BENEDICT:

　　　　Secret, Sister Luke?

SISTER LUKE:　Help me with my book-pages first. I'm folding my tent too. Like Saint Paul. Like you, Benedict.

(SISTER LUKE *gathers starched guimpes with the help of* SISTER BENEDICT *and makes a book-like bundle.*)

SISTER LUKE:　For my publisher! Will you look after this business for me? Please.

(SISTER BENEDICT *takes the bundle of guimpes.*)

SISTER BENEDICT:

　　　　Of course, Sister Luke. I promise.

SISTER LUKE:　Be careful not to lose it! Don't let anyone take it from you!

(SISTER LUKE *holds* SISTER BENEDICT *by the arm.*)

SISTER LUKE:　Listen to me now, Benedict. I'll tell you my secret!

　　　　When I jumped through that window, I escaped completely. So, I decided to continue on being the crazy nun, the duine le Dia. — Why should I give up my new freedom? — No more bowing and scraping to Mother Superiors. I can say whatever comes into my head.

　　　　I can mix toast into my porridge if I want to. Who made the rule that porridge must be eaten before toast? Who? — I can tell Central Powers the truth about themselves.

　　　　I can write my books.

　　　　I can be wherever I wish to be.

　　　　And still see my Angels and Archangels. Look! — They're all around us! There's Michael. He keeps Old Boy, Lucifer, far away from us. And Gabriel is shining brightly near the archway. So don't worry about Mother Victoire and her Rest Home, Benedict!

(SISTER BENEDICT *takes a book from her pocket.*)

SISTER BENEDICT:

I've brought you a book of poems. Your nephew's poems, Sister Luke. His photograph is here on the cover.

(SISTER LUKE *examines the book and looks steadily at the photograph.*)

SISTER LUKE: Bless you, Benedict. My nephew, the poet! Grandson of the golden-haired woman from the North.

Alleluia! Alleluia! —

SISTER BENEDICT:

You resemble him. Around the eyes. He has extraordinary eyes. Hasn't he?

SISTER LUKE: Yes! He must see Angels and Archangels too.

(SISTER LUKE *kisses the photograph.*)

SISTER BENEDICT:

Angels and Archangels.

(SISTER LUKE *opens book and turns pages.*)

SISTER LUKE: 'My father played the melodion,
My mother milked the cows,
And I had a prayer like a white rose pinned
On the Virgin Mary's blouse.'
My blessings go with you, Benedict!
Don't forget!

(*Pats bundle of guimpes.*)

SISTER BENEDICT:

Bless you, Sister, Luke!

(*She embraces* SISTER LUKE. *They kiss on both cheeks as* MOTHER VICTOIRE *enters.* MOTHER VICTOIRE *stands downstage right facing audience.*)

Sound: The Angelus Bell tolls.

(SISTER BENEDICT *moves centre stage, faces downstage.*)

MOTHER VICTOIRE:

Go straight to the Blue Parlour. Fold your habit and leave it with your guimpe, coif, rosary beads, belt and veil in the side-cupboard.

61

Your lay clothing is on a chair near the door. When you have dressed, go out immediately! Out the hall door! On no account are you to return to the cloister or to speak with any of the community. Your father and sister are waiting outside at the gate. —

(MOTHER VICTOIRE *stares at* SISTER BENEDICT.)

I hope you'll be happy.

SISTER BENEDICT:

Thank you, Mother Victoire. But, I'll keep this veil. My veil!

(SISTER BENEDICT *moves towards exit, turns to* SISTER LUKE *and waves goodbye.* MOTHER VICTOIRE *turns and sees* SISTER LUKE *wave to* SISTER BENEDICT, *who exits.* SISTER LUKE *then waves to* MOTHER VICTOIRE. *Lights change.* MOTHER VICTOIRE *exits.* SISTER LUKE *sits on chair-copter.*)

SISTER LUKE: Benedict's veil will spread and spread like Brigit of Kildare's cloak! Taking my book with it on all its journeys.

Benedict's people are in the book-publishing business for generations! —

Her great-uncle, Eugene Francis O'Brien, was very critical of Central Powers! His books were all banned in Ireland! I've a copy of his very first book. Banned too. A banned book in a convent! Shhh!

And Benedict's great-great uncles, Thomas Lewis O'Brien and Denis O'Brien, studied for the priesthood in St. Omer, a French seminary. During Penal Times.

But Thomas Lewis turned Protestant. — At one time he was Protestant rector in Templemichael, while his brother, Denis, was Roman Catholic priest in the same parish. In Ireland of course! — Strange but true! Thomas Lewis O'Brien wrote a lot of books. Plays and religious tracts.

You can find them all in the Big Dublin Library. —

He finished up as a Protestant Bishop in the North. —

(SISTER LUKE *stands and moves centre stage.*)

And by the way, that story I told you about Sister Benedict wanting to run away every morning she opened the Outside Gates. That was really about myself. —

When I was a young novice, I always wanted to run out through those Big Gates. Away! Away! But my parents! —

(*She turns and moves towards cloisters.*)

I wonder will my new book be banned?

Act 2 Scene 6

Lights up slowly to show the Lamentation over the dead Christ stained glass window upstage left.
Sound: Crashing sounds of demolition. Thunder of destruction.
SISTER LUKE *moves quickly towards walls as she tries to stop the collapse of walls and stained glass window.*

SISTER LUKE: Stop! Stop! That's my favourite window. My window! My window! (*Screams*) Stop! Stop! Father James help me! Help! Help! Save our window! — Sister Benedict! Sister Benedict come back and help me! — Angels and Archangels help! — Where are you, my Angels, my Archangels? God help! Please God! — Help save my window! My window! My window! Help! Help!

(*She raises her hands towards the window as a bull-dozer approaches.*)
SISTER LUKE: (*Screams*) No! No! No! Stop! Stop!
(SISTER LUKE *falls on floor as the window-wall begins to disintegrate. Use of special coloured lighting as broken (*plastic*) pieces fall from drop-box above stage.*
SISTER LUKE *picks up pieces of shattered glass.*)
Sound: Up slowly of *Lux Aeterna* from Mozart's *Requiem.*
SISTER LUKE: Job! Job! Help me now! Now! Now! Nobody comes! Nobody! Nobody!
(*The window-wall crashes on top of* SISTER LUKE. *She lies covered in stained glass. Noise of demolition fades. —*)
Sound: Fade *Lux Aeterna* from Mozart's *Requiem.*

Act 2 Scene 7

Lights with shadows.
Very little of the convent walls still standing. SISTER LUKE *sits on her chair-copter with guimpe-wings attached and takes pieces of stained glass from her pockets.*

SISTER LUKE: Epilogue. From my own favourite window. The colours are so gorgeous. — French ultramarines, crimsons, viridians, magentas! See how the light shines through them! — For Father James, when he returns. — Together we'll make a Resurrection Window from these broken pieces. My Angels and Archangels promise to help us.

(*She holds up pieces of stained glass to light.*)

Mother Victoire is in a Rest Home. There are no young novices to look after her. — But, she's happy most of the time.

(*Pause*)   They built a new wing for the convent museum. My photograph is displayed there beside a photograph of my nephew, the poet. Both in silver frames. — Alleluia! Alleluia! His Lordship himself came to perform the opening ceremony. All the way from Rome! Maura Ber from Harvard brought her book with the story of Katie and the rose medal. — A lovely party!
Lots of talk, photographs and plonk Champagne! But, a Bollinger Grande Année '76 Rosé for His Lordship!

(*Pause*)   They've cleaned up the convent cemetery. —
That commercial builder couldn't get
planning permission to exhume our remains
and build another multi-story car-park. —
So far! Alleluia!

(BENEDICT/BRIGIT O'BRIEN, *dressed as a business executive,
moves through cloisters and paints* SISTER LUKE'*s name on front of
small black cross.*)

Sister Benedict, now Brigit O'Brien, Managing
Director of O'Brien and Co. Publishers,
Dublin, London, Sydney, Auckland, Toronto
and New York, came here to transfer my
name, SISTER LUKE CAREY, from the
back to the front of that small iron cross. She
painted my name with her own hands.

(BRIGIT O'BRIEN *moves from cloister and places cross with name
centre downstage, kneels, makes sign of the cross, pauses, stands and
waves goodbye to grave as she exits.*)

Father James lives in Paris. At the Irish
College in Rue des Irlandais. He's busy
writing a book about those women, who
ministered to Christ during His public life.
He has a first edition of my own book.

(*Highlight on* SISTER LUKE.)

Sound: Fade in sound of *Benedictus* from Mozart's *Requiem
in D Minor.*

But every Easter Saturday Father James sends
me a bouquet of flowers, blue and crimson
edged with yellow and magenta. Colours of
the stained glass in La Chapelle.
By Interflora!
From Paris. — Alleluia! Alleluia!

Sound up: *Benedictus* from Mozart's *Requiem in D Minor.*
THE LINES:
Benedictus qui venit in nomine Domini.
Repeated by:
Soprano, alto, tenor and bass with orchestra.

Highlight on SISTER LUKE *in chair, then fade light as tableau forms showing* FATHER JAMES *down left beside stained glass window,* THE BISHOP OF KILLMACHA *upstage from window,* MOTHER VICTOIRE, BRIGIT O'BRIEN *and* MAURA BER *stand in spaces between cloister-columns. Lights up for two beats then fade to black.*

END

Music in S<small>TAINED</small> G<small>LASS</small> AT S<small>AMHAIN</small>

P<small>RE</small>-L<small>IGHTS</small> U<small>P</small>: *Benedictus* from Mozart's *Requiem in D Minor*
(No. 12 on CD)
Soprano, Alto, Tenor and Bass with Orchestra.
Benedictus qui venit in nomine Domini —
Sung by: Magdaléna Hajóssyová, Soprano;
Jaroslava Horská, Alto; Josef Kundlák, Tenor
& Peter Mikulás, Bass
with Slovak Philharmonic Orchestra and Chorus
(Mozart's *Requiem* completed by Sussmayr.)

A<small>CT</small> 1 S<small>CENE</small> 5: Top of scene. Ticking clock before alarm
clock rings
Angelus bell tolls. Fast convent bell sounds.

A<small>CT</small> 1 S<small>CENE</small> 7: Sister Luke and Maura Ber sing *Seothín,
seo hó* echoing one another.

A<small>CT</small> 1 S<small>CENE</small> 11:(End of scene) *Agnus Dei* from
Mozart's *Requiem*.

A<small>CT</small> 2 S<small>CENE</small> 1: *I Dreamt I Dwelt in Marble Halls*
sung by Méav

A<small>CT</small> 2 S<small>CENE</small> 1: (Towards end of scene) *I Dreamt I Dwelt in
Marble Halls*

A<small>CT</small> 2 S<small>CENE</small> 2: (End of scene) Mass bell tolls followed by
Kyrie Eleison from *The Greatest Ornament*
sung by Nóirín Ní Riain, with shruti box
and male choir. (19 & 20) on to

A<small>CT</small> 2 S<small>CENE</small> 3: *Magnificat cum Alleluia*
sung by Nóirín Ní Riain (39)

A<small>CT</small> 2 S<small>CENE</small> 3: *The Limestone Rock*
played by Micho Russell. (2)
(Continue sound over until end of scene.)

A<small>CT</small> 2 S<small>CENE</small> 5: Angelus bell tolls. (Towards end of scene.)

A<small>CT</small> 2 S<small>CENE</small> 6: *Lux Aeterna* from Mozart's *Requiem*

A<small>CT</small> 2 S<small>CENE</small> 7: End of performance: *Benedictus in nomine Domini*
as at beginning of performance.

Other Plays by Patricia Burke Brogan

Credo   A Monologue
Requiem   Two-Act Play
Yours Truly   Two-Act Play
Cell   Radio Play
Ladies' Day   Verse Play

TRILOGY OF PLAYS
Eclipsed   Two-Act Play
Clarenda's Mirror   Three-Act Play
The Generous Imposter   Work-in-Progress Play

PLAYS FOR CHILDREN
Rehearsal For A Miracle   One-Act Play
Boats Can Fly   One-Act Play

SCREEN PLAYS
Custody Of The Eyes
Seen and Unseen

About the Playwright

PATRICIA BURKE BROGAN is a painter, poet and playwright. Her etchings have won awards at Barcelona and at Listowel International Biennale 1982. *Above the Waves Calligraphy*, her collection of poems and etchings, and the script of her stage play, *Eclipsed*, were published by Salmon Publishing in 1994. *Eclipsed* has won many awards including a Fringe First at Edinburgh Theatre Festival 1992 and the USA Moss Hart Award 1994. To date there have been fifty-three productions of the play on three continents. *Eclipsed* has been excerpted in documentaries and other collected works including *The Field Day Anthology of Irish Writing*, Volumes 4 and 5, *Irish Women Playwrights of the Twentieth Century*, *Ireland's Women: Writings Past and Present*, and *Motherhood in Ireland*. Patricia received an Arts Council Bursary in Literature in 1993 and a European Script Writers' Fund in 1994.